WANTED !!!

3 guys to form a band

1 charismatic vocalist
(Knowledge of current affairs
would be an advantage)

1 enigmatic axeman

1 bass player (preferably
extroverted and outgoing)

Contact Larry, Class 3A

The Legend of U2

By Scratch & Kerr

And Other Things Besides

ANNA LIVIA P·R·E·S·S

**Scratch's political cartoons
appear in the Evening Herald.**

Published by Anna Livia Press Ltd,
21 Cross Avenue, Dún Laoghaire, Co. Dublin
ISBN 1-871311-03-9

Designed by Brendan Foreman/The Graphiconies
Cover: Bluett
Set in Bodoni and Futura by Amadeus Publications Ltd.
Printed by The Guernsey Press Ltd.

Illustrations copyright © 1989 by Aongus Collins
Original text copyright © 1989 by Colin Kerr

Sources
We'd like to acknowledge the following books: *Unforgettable Fire*, by Eamon Dunphy
(Penguin, 1988); *U2: Touch The Flame*, by Geoff Parkin (Omnibus Press, 1987); *Irish Rock*,
by Mark Prendergast (O'Brien Press, 1987); *U2 — Rattle & Hum* (Pyramid Books, 1988);
The U2 File, ed Niall Stokes (Hot Press, 1985).
Back issues of the *Hot Press* were thumbed heavily; we also consulted *Q*, *Rolling Stone*, *NME*
and *Melody Maker*.
Finally thanks to Maurice Haugh & his video.

"Care for a test drive, sir?"

PROLOGUE

U2 *Shame*

The history of rock'n'roll has been fairly sordid at the best of times but in terms of gross, obscene, flaccid, stomach churning ugliness nothing has matched the ultimate horror of Progressive Rock.

Progressive Rock meant no fun. Its idea of a good time was to record a triple album every three years, write a book about the concept, go on tour for the next three years and then wait for the record company to come up with another gatefold sleeve before going back into the studio.

It called itself Yes, Jethro Tull, Emerson, Lake & Palmer, King Crimson, Pink Floyd, The Moody Blues, Uriah Heep and it didn't release singles.

It should have been a stockbroker, an accountant or an architect but lacked the talent to do any of these things. Progressive Rock was the final degradation of rock'n'roll. If there is an afterlife, particularly unpleasant criminals may end up in a small room listening to *Olias of Sunhillow* outakes for all eternity as a group of progressive rock students clad in elephant flares and t-shirts with stars on them earnestly explain the concept, man.

AGM of the Gary Glitter Appreciation Society.

U2 *Chirpy Chirpy Cheap*

Remember Middle Of The Road, Dawn, Little Jimmy Osmond, Boney M, Lena Zavaroni? No? God, you're lucky.

Pop music sunk to new depths in the Seventies. There was teeny pop, tartan pop, Euro pop, wombling and myriad lesser art forms that the industry packaged for an infantile market.

Some of the records were so bad, they've since become collectors' items.

If you've any of the following tracks in your racks you should seek help. You could also become very rich.

• My Friend The Wind — Demis Roussos
• Sugar Baby Love — The Rubettes
• The Smurf Song — Father Abraham
• Ma, He's Making Eyes At Me — Lena Zavaroni
• I Am A Cider Drinker — The Wurzles
• Amazing Grace — The Pipes and Drums and Military Band of the Scots Dragoon
• Seasons In The Sun — Terry Jacks
• Honey — Bobby Goldsboro
• Rasputin — Boney M
• Tie A Yellow Ribbon — Dawn
• The Floral Dance — Brighouse and Rastrick Brass Dance
• Save Your Kisses For Me — Brotherhood of Man
• Day Trip To Bangor — Fiddlers Dram
• Chirpy Chirpy Cheep Cheep — Middle Of The Road
• Long Haired Lover From Liverpool — Little Jimmy Osmond
• Puppy Love — Donny Osmond
• Paper Roses — Marie Osmond
• Morning Side Of The Mountain — Marie and Donny Osmond

U2 *Only Gorgeous*

Then came Glam Rock. It started when Marc Bolan, the creator of *My People Were Fair and Had Sky In Their Hair But Now They're Content To Wear Stars On Their Brows*, changed the name of his ensemble from Tyrannosaurus Rex to T. Rex (allegedly because BBC Radio One DJs couldn't pronounce tyrannosaurus.)
Bolan sprinkled glitter dust on his make-up and the rest is history: platform shoes, sequined jackets, lurex suits, gold lamé cloaks and some of the greatest pop music ever written.

GLAM ROCK AT A GLANCE

Artiste	Trademark
David Bowie	Androgyny
Roxy Music	Melancholy
Sweet	"And the man in the back said everyone attack . . ."
Slade	Noize and hevvy lyrics
Mott The Hoople	"All the young Doo-whoodes . . ."
Sparks	Charlie Chaplin and a diva
Suzi Quatro	Leather
Gary Glitter	The leader of the Gang

For a short while glam became Art, epitomised by David Bowie's inspired imitation of a carrot.
He started off as a space cadet on *Space Oddity*, then transmogrified into Joan of Arc *(Hunky Dory)* before becoming the notorious Ziggy Stardust. Bowie announced his retirement in July '73.

11

"And then he said, 'Hit me with your rhythm stick, hit me, hit me.' . . . "

U2 *Savage Messiah*

Who was the first punk? Some say Iggy Pop, others still Frank Sinatra. There are even those who have thrown Bing Crosby's name into the ring.

But the man who probably did more than anybody else to change the face of the rock industry for at least five minutes was John Lydon.

His friends called him Johnny Rotten because of his aversion to toothbrushes and his all consuming hatred of the dental profession. Also he snarled and sneered a lot.

In November '75 the Sex Pistols played their first ever concert at St Martin's College of Art in Hornsby, North London. After ten minutes they were asked to leave because they didn't know any Yes songs.

A year later 50 people turned up to see them at the 100 Club in London. Among them were some talent scouts who'd survived the excesses of the early Seventies and were looking for the future of rock'n'roll.

They still hadn't found what they were looking for. But for the time being, at least, the Pistols (as they were known to their friends and those in the business) would do nicely.

EMI, home of The Beatles, was the first company to fall for the discreet charm of the punk anti-Christs and their Machiavellian manager, Malcolm McLaren. In November '76 the Pistols released the teen anthem, *Anarchy in the UK*, and two months later were given a £40,000 kiss-off by EMI. EMI's feet chilled after the Pistols mouthed rude words on television.

By March '77 in an attempt to clean

up their image the band had recruited John Beverly, a quiet spoken youngster who sometimes called himself Sid Vicious.

The fab four then signed to A&M Records at a photo opportunity outside Buckingham Palace. Nine days later they received £75,000 redundancy money.

Enter Richard Branson and Virgin. Branson had made his fortune by championing the boy genius and all 'round tedious bore Mike Oldfield. In May the Pistols released *God Save the Queen* to coincide with the Royal jubilee celebrations.

Pretty Vacant and *Holidays In The Sun* were followed by their only LP *Never Mind The B******s* which entered the UK album charts at number one in November.

Two months later Johnny Rotten decided he'd had enough. He fronted the band for the last time at the Winterland Ballroom in

San Francisco.

The others soldiered on minus Rotten (now Lydon again) and in June '78 joined forces with Great Train Robber Ronnie Biggs on *No One Is Innocent*. Biggs later complained that he hadn't received payment for the record; he protested that he'd been ripped off.

In February '79, Sid Vicious who'd been charged with the murder of his girlfriend Nancy Spungen died from a heroin overdose in a Greenwich Village flat.

The demise of punk was confirmed officially on June 30, '79 when John Lydon appeared on Juke Box Jury with Joan Collins.

Bands like Blondie, The Clash, The Buzzcocks, The Jam and The Stranglers continued to carry the flag and Lydon formed a new band Public Image Limited.

But punk without the Pistols was like Hamlet without the prince. No future.

"Short back and sides, please."

U2 *Sham Rock*

In Ireland new wave bands had names like The Radiators From Space, The Gamblers, The Boy Scoutz, The Vipers, The Kamikaze Kids, Revolver and The Sinners. But only one man had the energy, the vision and lack of conventional musical talent to follow the British punk giants. Geldof, Bob Geldof: the South Dublin voice of a generation. Geldof had a dream, a dream that he shared with thousands of Irish youngsters who were only dying to get on Top Of The Pops.

"I'm into pop music because I want to get rich, get famous and get laid," he explained. A string of hits followed for the Boomtown Rats.

In 1978 *Rat Trap* spent 15 weeks in the charts, two weeks at number one toppling John Travolta and Olivia Newton John's *Summer Nights*. To celebrate, Geldof ceremoniously shredded a pin-up poster of the duo on the Thursday night chart show. A year later the Rats were back at number one with *I Don't Like Mondays*. It was the true story of an American schoolgirl who shot her schoolmates because she didn't like Mondays. That simple. 'Trouble was, American stations boycotted the song because of alleged poor taste. But *Mondays* was the Rats' finest hour . . . and an inspiration to fledgling Irish bands.

15

THE LEGEND

U2 — The Original Line-Up

1 Flann O'Brien
2 Ronnie Drew
3 Van Morrison
4 W. B. Yeats
5 Nietzsche
  (couldn't find a decent reference)
6 David Bowie
7 John Lennon
8 Bob Geldof
9 Adam Clayton
10 The Edge

11 Bono
12 Larry Mullen
13 Rolf Harris
14 Bruce Springsteen
15 B. B. King
16 Elvis
17 Mick Jagger
18 Frank Sinatra
19 Jack Charlton
20 John Lydon
21 Jimi Hendrix

22 Paul Rowen
23 Lou Reed
24 Keith Richards
25 A Bay City Roller
26 Paul McGuinness
27 Bob Dylan
28 Patti Smith
29 Charles J. Haughey
30 Debbie Harry

U2 *Pro Bono Publico*

Paul Hewson was destined to be leader of the most successful band ever to come out of Ireland. Born on May 10, 1960 he lived in Cedarwood Avenue, Ballymun, in the heart of Dublin's northside.

He dreamt of being an Indian. "At school," he explained, "I was always with the Indians. I think the cowboys always had it too easy — always the good guys, always the winners." After school he would hang around with his friends from Lypton Village, a mythical Indian reservation populated by his friends, Gavin, Strongman, Dave Id, Guggi and Pod. They all had funny names because it sounded like a good idea at the time. Legend has it that Bono got his name from the hearing aid shop in O'Connell Street, Bonovox. Bono he has been ever since.

Bono is now married to Ali with a child called Jordan, named presumably after the Biblical river. His interests include world events, the arts, hairstyles and meeting people. "The whole political picture right now is completely outmoded," he says. "The Right and the Left are ridiculous — they don't mean anything anymore. These are old ideologies. You can learn from Marx, you can learn from Lenin — but my worry is: why are there no new Marxes or Lenins? Why is there such a void in political thinking at the moment? Why are we using solutions to problems of an industrial revolution when we're going through our own revolutions — technological, ideological, everything-ological?" Why indeed? Bonoism, an ideology for the 1990s.

U2 *Toil and Stubble*

At nine he started playing a guitar
which his mother bought in a jumble
sale for £1. At ten he bought his first
cowboy hat. At 11 he started shaving.
At 11.05 he stopped.

This was The Edge, Evans the axe.
Dave Evans was born on August 8
1961 in Barking East London.

His parents were Welsh. They didn't
like Barking. So they moved to the
leafy Dublin suburb of Malahide in
1962. By the time Dave reached
Mount Temple comprehensive school
his guitar skills were finely tuned, or
so legend has it, by Beatles guitar
duets with his brother Dick, an early
member of the U2 prototype band
The Hype and later of the The Virgin
Prunes.

After a few years in Mount Temple,
Dave became known to his friends as
The Edge. But his really close friends
called him The.

The Edge is the quiet man of U2. "My life revolves around the music, the keyboard. My family should make a difference but I'm not able to spend enough time with them," he once revealed in a rare outburst of loquaciousness.

The Edge is married to Aislinn and has three daughters, Holly, Aaron and Blue. Sometimes he plays the piano and he likes reading Raymond Carver books. His ambition is to re-invent rock'n'roll.

"The Edge is a really intense guy, he's got this incredibly high IQ," says Bono. "He's great at sorting out issues of world importance, it's just that he forgets the everyday things like the chords of songs, where he is and so on."

U2 *Boys wanna have fun*

He's the oldest member of the band. Adam was born on March 13, 1960 in Chinnor, Oxfordshire. At the age of five, he moved with his family to the leafy Dublin suburb of Malahide.

In his early years Adam had problems adapting to the Irish educational system. An early report from Castle Park preparatory school called him a "chatterbox". At St Columba's College, Rathfarnham, he got into trouble for not wearing the school uniform. Then he went to Mount Temple.

At Mount Temple, where a liberal ethic prevailed, Adam amused himself by drinking coffee in the classroom and occasionally streaking through the corridors.

After a while he was asked to leave. He bought his first guitar in a

quayside shop for £12. This was replaced later by a nifty looking bass guitar which cost £52.

He also spent a month on the hippy trail in Pakistan and possessed an Afghan coat. After he got his first bass, he told his parents, "I'll play till I'm bigger than the Beatles."

Adam likes reggae, nightclubs, parties and more parties. He is not married and has no children.

Adam is the wild man of U2 — but that's still pretty polite by most rock'n'roll standards.

"We're not the biggest rooting tooting drinking rock'n'roll band in the world," he once confessed. "I mean we're fairly level-headed and sober most of the time. That helps, the fact that you aren't constantly out of it. It does blur very very easily."

U2 *Our Founder*

Larry, Boy Wonder to Bono's
Batman, changed the face of
rock'n'roll in autumn 1976 when he
stuck a note on the Mount Temple
school noticeboard, looking for
people to form a band.

Larry was born on October 31, 1961.
He was reared in Rosemount Avenue,
Artane. His education started at the
all Irish-speaking college Scoil Naomh
Colmchille and after school he'd go
for piano lessons to the Dublin
College of Music in Chatham Street.
He didn't like the piano so he started
playing the drums instead.

He tried to join the Artane Boys
Band, but they told him his hair was
too long.

He got it cut but it was still too long.
So Larry cut his losses and left. He
joined the Post Office Workers Union
band and travelled around Ireland
with them, his first experience of life
on the road.

By now he had a proper drum kit and
used to practise at home after
watching bands like The Sweet, The
Glitter Band and Slade on TV.

Solo drumming has a limited appeal;

hence the fateful notice on the school noticeboard. (A copy of the original notice is thought to be hidden somewhere in the vaults of the National Museum.)

Bono says his earliest memory of Larry was when they were at their first rehearsal in his kitchen. Girls kept climbing over the walls and looking in the window at Larry. Larry shouted and told them to go away. But they wouldn't so he turned the hose on them.

"All the sex and drugs in rock is so old, so boring and so pretentious," says Larry.

Larry hates giving interviews or having his picture taken. He's a sex symbol in Japan where he's popularly known as "Lalee". Millions of Larry Mullen t-shirts are sold all over Ireland every year. He likes Harley Davidson motorbikes. He is not married and has no nickname but is called Larry Mullen Jnr to distinguish him from his father Larry Snr who tired of receiving exorbitant tax demands intended for his son.

U2 *Taurus*

Bono was born on 10 May, 1960, under the sign of the bull. Soothsayers reckon Taureans to be pretty okay people, give or take a stubborn streak, which is offset by a generous nature.

On the day Bono uttered his first cry, the news was dominated by another U2 . . . the American U2 spy-plane flown by Gary Powers, which had been shot down over the USSR on May Day. The Soviet Union was notifying the United States that Powers would be brought to account under the laws of the USSR.

In Ireland, violence hit the headlines as masked men blew up an Orange Hall in Mount Forest, Co. Tyrone.

That week the excellent Everly Brothers were at number one in the British charts with the sublime *Cathy's Clown*. And in the US, Elvis ruled the charts with *Stuck On You*. Bono shares his birthday with Denis Thatcher, Donovan, and Irish boxer, Charlie Nash.

U2 *Leo*

According to savants, your typical Leo will have a larger than life personality, an imposing presence and a highly extroverted nature.

The Edge is one, born on 8 August, 1961. On that day, the Queen of England and the Duke of Edinburgh paid a visit to Belfast.

Internationally, the Cold War had reached an ominous pitch and Russian defence workers were reported to have asked their government for permission to work longer hours to strengthen Soviet defences.

In Hollywood, it was confirmed that Judy Garland had separated from husband, Sid Luft, and was seeking a divorce.

Helen Shapiro topped the British Hit Parade with *You Don't Know*, while Bobby Lewis had a number one in the USA with *Tossin' and Turnin'*.

The Edge shares his birthday with Dustin Hoffman, Connie Stevens and Nigel Mansell.

 *Pisces*

Adam was born on 13 March, 1960, which makes him a Piscean. Many people hold that Pisceans are sensitive, mystical, elusive, self-consciously charismatic and send out amazing vibes.

Adam was born on a so-so sort of day, newswise. Kruschev postponed a two week visit to France because he had the flu.

Back in Ireland, sheep farmers in Co. Mayo had plenty to worry about. Such was the damage being done by killer dogs roaming the countryside, the local priests were asked to read out warning notices at Mass.

Adam Faith was at number one in the British charts with *Poor Me*. In the US, Percy Faith's *Theme From A Summer Place* completed its third week at the top; it stayed there for a massive nine weeks.

Adam shares his birthday with Neil Sedaka and British heavyweight boxer, Joe Bugner.

U2 *Scorpio*

Larry is a Scorpio. Scorpios are absolutely top of the heap, according to astrologers. Their essential traits can be described only with recourse to a string of over-the-top superlatives.

On 31 October, 1961, Larry was born. That day, the Russians decided that Stalin's body should be removed from the Lenin mausoleum and taken to the wall of the Kremlin on account of his crimes.

In Ireland, young Gardaí were meeting to organise a campaign for better pay.

In the UK, Helen Shapiro was number one in the charts with that celebrated belter, *Walking Back To Happiness*. In the US, Dion was at the top with *Runaround Sue*.

Larry shares his birthday with Tom Paxton, Eddie Charlton and Jimmy Saville.

The site of Dublin's legendary Dandelion Market where U2 played their legendary early gigs.

The Man Who Knew U2 When They Were Nothing.

U2 *Desire*

The U2 story starts in Larry Mullen's kitchen in Rosemount Avenue. They had one set of drums, one bass without an amp, one borrowed electric guitar and one borrowed amplifier. Present were Larry, Adam, The Edge, Bono, and various other hopefuls who now tell their friends that they were members of the original U2.

At the last count approximately 546 people were present. But most left because they thought that Larry, Adam, The Edge and Bono were useless and going nowhere.

The Lost and Alleged members of U2 can be found in pubs all over Dublin and will tell you that the band is still brutal. Larry was the original leader but Bono took over five minutes into the first rehearsal.

At this time they were called Feedback and played *Brown Sugar* and *Satisfaction* because Bono thought he was Mick Jagger.

When they played their first concert at a school talent concert in Mount Temple their set included a version of Peter Frampton's *Show Me The Way* and songs by The Beach Boys and The Bay City Rollers.

Feedback is probably one of the worst names any rock group ever had. So it was hardly surprising that in 1977 the hottest band on the leafy Malahide Road changed their name to The Hype.

Still that didn't exactly trip off the tongue. On the advice of Dublin punk guru Steve Averill (aka Steve Rapid of the Radiators From Space) they became U2.

In early 1978 The Hype played their last concert in a community centre. With a fine sense of rock'n'roll history they played the first half of the show as The Hype with The Edge's brother Dick on guitar and the second half minus Dik as U2.

Dik went on to join The Virgin Prunes (featuring Lypton Village minus Bono) and soon Dublin was covered in graffiti saying, "U2 Can Become A Virgin Prune".

There was a healthy rivalry between U2 and the Prunes to see who could become the biggest band since The Beatles.

And the Prunes were present in the audience that travelled to Limerick to see U2 compete in a talent contest and play a storming set to capture the £500 first prize, courtesy of Harp Lager.

Now all they needed was a manager. On the advice of rock journalist Bill Graham they contacted one Paul McGuinness.

 McGuinness is good for U2

Paul McGuinness once managed a folk-rock combo called Spud. Not many people know that. But Spud weren't destined to be a band that people knew much about.

The fifth member of U2 was born on June 16, 1951 in Rinteln near Hanover, West Germany, where his father, an RAF pilot, was stationed. At the age of ten he arrived in Dublin to study at the posh Clongowes Wood College. Then off to Trinity College Dublin where he did a bit of acting, philosophy and psychology.

After a row with a college official over an allegedly libellous article in a student magazine he headed for London where he spent some time working as a taxi driver.

In '72 he was back in Dublin working as an assistant location manager on the "interesting" John Boorman film *Zardoz* after which he worked as assistant director on various television commercials.

When asked to manage Spud, he jumped at the chance. After a year of moderate success they parted company.

In May '78 he spoke to U2 after a gig and agreed to manage them.

He dressed in a suit. He spoke well. He looked like a businessman. And he actually believed that bands should get paid for working.

In those days, financial arrangements were usually quite informal. Some promoters would offer to pay a band's busfares home and promise them a return booking with better money at some unspecified future date.

McGuinness did not appreciate such arrangements and tried to make sure that U2 avoided the local flea pits as much as possible.

Today one of the wealthiest men in Ireland, he is courted by many industrialists and politicians. So far he has not agreed to manage any of them.

U2 *World Domination*

In September '78, U2 supported The Stranglers at the Top Hat ballroom outside Dublin.

By this time they'd become objects of derision among the Dublin punk fraternity. They spoke with posh accents, their manager was a businessman and worst of all they were supporting real punk bands. When U2 went on that night some punks screamed at Bono and called him a poseur. He pleaded with them to give the band a chance. He was told to f**k off.

Such abuse proved to be no more than a hiccup. More Dublin gigs followed and in February '79 U2 played a 24 hour punk festival, Dark Space (BBC radio punk guru, John Peel, was there; he didn't think they were very good).

But CBS Ireland liked them. A month after Dark Space, U2 signed to the label after British record companies had said thanks but no thanks.

In September they released the single *U2 3* featuring *Out Of Control*, *Stories For Boys*, and *Boy Girl*. It sold 1,000 copies in Ireland.

Around this time two English record company talent scouts came to Dublin to watch the band.

Half way through the gig in a Dublin pub they left to view another hot happening band . . . on the Old Grey Whistle Test, back in their hotel. They never signed U2 and the other band has since split up.

An A&R man from a different company was flown over to Ireland to check out U2. But he got drunk and missed the gig. Desperate to return to London with something to show for his efforts, he signed a lesser Dublin band which disappeared without trace.

U2 *Hope and Glory*

Within three years, U2 were Ireland's most-likely-to-succeed band, its most happening band . . . in short, its next Boomtown Rats.

All that remained was to conquer the rest of the world.

In December '79 the band set out on their first, and not exactly triumphal, UK tour. The low point was a gig in the Hope and Anchor attended by nine people.

But back home they were still only mega. Their second single *Another Day* (on CBS Ireland) brought more kudos and applause from a growing army of followers.

By March '80 U2 were big enough to quit the pubs, clubs and backstreet basements. They played their first gig in Dublin's National Stadium. In the audience was a rep from Island Records.

Island was founded in '62 by Chris Blackwell, a shy music loving businessman. At first it specialised in releasing imported West Indies discs. Its first platter was *Twist Baby* by Owen Gray. (Millie Small of *My Boy Lollipop* fame was managed by Blackwell.)

During the Sixties, Blackwell went on to sign some major bores . . . King Crimson, Cat Stevens and ELP among them. In the Seventies, though, he kept better company: Roxy Music, the early Mott the Hoople, Bob Marley and a roster of impressive reggae musicians.

In the Eighties he was still looking for the big one. After the Stadium gig the word came back that U2 were indeed that one. "U2 are the label's most important signing since King Crimson," he declared when they signed along the dotted line.

An Cat Dubh

Traumas of boyhood.

 *Oh Boy!*

U2's first Island single, *11 O'Clock Tick Tock*, was produced by Martin Hannett, an avant garde Mancunian ahead of his time and possibly everybody else's as well.

Nobody bought the record, i.e. it's a collector's item.

Enter Steve Lillywhite who at the wholesome age of 25 had made a name and a lot of money for himself producing Souxsie and the Banshees, Ultravox, and Eddie and the Hot Rods.

He oversaw the next single, *A Day Without Me*, which was catchier than *Tick Tock*, huge in Ireland and a flop everywhere else.

Undaunted, the band went into Windmill Lane Studios to start on the album, *Boy*. The LP is mainly about the condition of boyhood and the leaving thereof. The title gives a valuable clue in this regard, as does the cover which features a photo of a young boy.

Peter Rowen, brother of Guggi of the Virgin Prunes, made his debut on the sleeve of the first U2 single, *U2 3*, when he was only five years old.

He was six when he adorned the cover of *Boy*. Two years later, he appeared on the cover of *WAR*.

Peter went on to U2's old alma mater Mount Temple and developed a passion for Bob Dylan and skateboarding. He's 15 years old now.

"We put him on the cover because he's a pretty smart kid," explained Bono after the release of their début album, "and sometimes I wonder what his future will be like . . . and I wonder about ours."

Boy reached number 52 in the UK album charts. Maybe it wasn't a runaway, runaway success but it put U2 on the map.

After the album's release in October '80 the band started a major British tour and played their first European shows in Belgium and Holland.

In November they returned from the Continent and started their first American tour, performing at clubs on the East Coast and laying the foundations for their future conquest of the US.

U2 *Faith*

In '79, Pope John Paul II came to Ireland and uttered the immortal words:

"Young People of Ireland. I Love U2."

Not that long ago Ireland saw itself as the most Catholic country in Europe. But that was before the pagan Pandora's Box of the Sixties was opened on national television. Suddenly governments were legalising the use of contraceptives and liberals were pushing for divorce.

The Pope took the opportunity to lay traditional teaching on morals on the line. The faithful were told to get back on their knees.

A rather different spiritual movement was building up elsewhere. Three quarters of U2 were committed heavily to Christianity.

Back in Mount Temple, Bono had been in the school's Christian Union and went to Saturday morning prayer meetings. When Pod and Guggi from Lypton Village became involved in a charismatic Christian group called Shalom, he went along. Soon he was joined by The Edge and Larry. Meanwhile Adam pursued an entirely different personal vision elsewhere. At prayer meetings each week, the three sang gospel songs. They brought Bibles on tour and held prayer meetings in hotel rooms. Most rock groups wrecked hotels. U2 sanctified them.

And while others sang of S&D&R'n'R, Bono sang of salvation. Especially on the band's second album. *October* looks like a rock album, it sounds like a rock album but it's really a collection of hymns played with electric guitar. Bono even sang bits of it in Latin, the language of liturgy.

The record was finished in an unholy panic, however, since Bono had lost all the lyrics and musical ideas for the album while touring the 'States. He ended up making up some of the words as he stood in front of the microphone. In places *October* sounds like a rant from an evangelical street preacher.

After it was released, Bono, The Edge and Larry suffered a spiritual crisis.

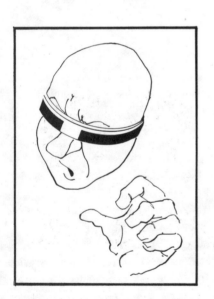

They concluded that they could not be Christians and rock'n'rollers at the same time. They decided to concentrate on their Christian vision at the expense of rock'n'roll.

They broke the news to McGuinness who reminded them that they had responsibilities to their record company, their road crew and promoters who had already booked them for gigs to promote *October*.

They agreed to stay in the band but the dilemma remains . . . except for Adam, a freer spirit. Years later Bono joked: "What has kept us together? Fear of our manager!"

This quasi-religious mixture of fear and faith has transformed U2 into a modern Irish economic miracle.

In June '81, U2 had their first British chart single with *Fire*. In October the second single from the album, *Gloria*, made it two-in-a-row. And *October* charted at number 11 in the album charts on its first week of release. Within a month it had earned the band their first silver disc.

After a British and American tour U2 saw in the new year with a Dublin concert attended by 5,000 fans and some begrudgers. Later that month U2 returned to America to complete the *October* tour supporting the J Geils Band along the way.

In March '82 *A Celebration* gave the band a hat trick of UK hit singles. That summer Bono married Ali Stewart, his girlfriend since Mount Temple, with Adam as best man. The couple honeymooned in Jamaica. U2 spent the autumn writing *WAR* and then went back into the studios with Steve Lillywhite.

"Did the earth move for you, too?"

Bono converts St Patrick

Sting saves the whales.

"This week's charts – Apartheid falls one place to 3, Central America moves up one to 2 and we have a new No. 1 – The Brazilian Rainforest!"

U2's politics at a glance*

Good	Not Good
Social Justice	Nuclear Devastation
Openness	Torture of Political Prisoners
Spirituality	Ecological destruction
Fair Play	South American dictators
World Peace	Rock sponsorship
Greens	War
Roots	Terrorism
Love	Oppression

* Further elucidation coming to a concert near you.

U2 *The Real Taoiseach*

"In Ireland he is regarded with awe. Many even see him as a future Prime Minister of a country where half the population is under 25."

This assessment of Bono's future career prospects comes from a British tabloid. It's a bit dodgy as the Taoiseach's salary is a paltry £65,796 a year.

Bono's domestic policies include more investment in the health service, the preservation of historic buildings, a more equitable tax system, the ending of the IRA's terrorist campaign and the withdrawal of British troops from Northern Ireland.

In the area of foreign policy he supports nuclear disarmament, economic sanctions against South Africa, the release of political prisoners and the ending of American involvement in Nicaragua and El Salvador.

"The re-mix didn't work out as expected."

"Eureka! The operation turned out just as you specified, Mr. Jackson."

U2 *Declaring WAR*

Every so often somebody pops up and becomes the voice of a generation. In the Fifties, there was Elvis. The Sixties had Dylan, the Beatles and the Stones. In the Seventies you couldn't believe anything anybody said.
Until *WAR* no Eighties band made a credible stab at spokespersonship for that generation.
The album declared war on oppression, terrorism, racism, exploitation and nuclear annihilation. And it identified the enemy.
The enemy called themselves "New Romantics". They dressed expensively in floppy suits and hairstyles. They posed for *The Face*. They affected a melancholy gaze.

And they released synthesiser-based dirges, accompanied by videos of themselves in expensive floppy suits and hairstyles, posing in an indefinably melancholy way.
Then they wept all the way to the bank.
"The band is hitting out against all the blippety bop aural wallpaper we have crammed down our throats on the radio and TV every day. I am personally bloody sick of every time I switch on the radio of being blasted with this contrived crap," raged Bono.
Deliberately, they stripped their sound to "bare bones and knuckles and three capital letters, W.A.R . . . "

"*WAR* is a slap in the face. We wanted an album that would separate us from our contemporaries."
As U2 were recording *WAR*, parliamentary opposition leader Garret FitzGerald dropped into Windmill Lane for a general election photo-opportunity with Bono and the lads.
Undoubtedly, Bono told Garret how to run the country. What Garret told Bono isn't known and was probably indecipherable in any case.
FitzGerald won the election.
WAR was released in February '83 and yielded two hit singles — *New Years Day* and *Two Hearts Beat as One*. It crashed into the UK album

charts at number 1, blasting Michael Jackson's *Thriller* off the top spot. The next month U2 began a three-month tour of America. Within a month *WAR* entered the US top ten and the band got their first American gold record. The tour finished with U2 playing a series of stadium gigs to more than 10,000 people a night. *WAR* was followed by a spectacular tour, captured in the video *Under A Blood Red Sky* which shows the rain sodden Red Rocks stadium being transformed into the Venice of America.

It was around this time that Bono started brandishing a large white flag. Discerning audiences realised that U2

Do the Bono

were not entirely in favour of military conflict.

In November '83 *Under A Blood Red Sky*, U2's first live album, entered the UK charts at number two and went platinum the following January. That same month *WAR* notched up its twelfth consecutive month in the UK charts.

U2 were now flavour of the month and on their way to become an awesomely monstrous stadium band. Chris Blackwell smiled . . . which is more than could be said of the forbidding photo of Peter Rowen which was used as a backdrop for each stage performance.

"First, we're gonna do something about your acne."

"He's still living back in the Sixties."

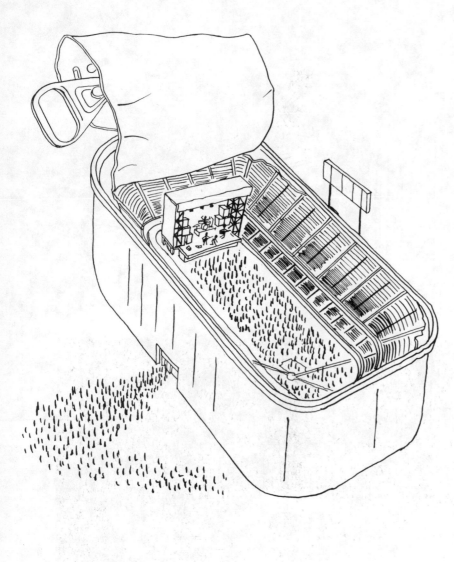

**Bono as seen from
the back row of a
baseball stadium.**

U2 *Stadium Fright*

The best rock'n'roll is played in small dingy basements where you have to walk past the stage to get to the toilets and run the risk of getting clobbered by a flailing guitar if you don't watch your step.

This is where U2 served their apprenticeship on their way to becoming the ultimate stadium band. "People are quite aware," said Bono, "that there's no stage big enough for me — I like to stretch the stage and I've often found myself singing from the back of the hall rather than the front. I'm always trying to communicate."

Most bands and their crews devote a lot of energy to keeping fans off the stage. With U2, the problem is keeping Bono out of the audience.

In March '83 in Los Angeles Bono jumped from a height of 20 feet into the 12,000 strong audience.

During the *WAR* tour he'd scale the scaffolding like a mountaineer, marking his triumphant ascent by planting a white flag at the top. Stadium rock is also usually very loud. In October '84 while playing in Brussels U2 set off the city's super sensitive seismographic earthquake measuring equipment.

During the *Joshua Tree* tour, U2 had up to 70 people in their road crew. The first leg of their American tour cost an estimated £5 million.

They own their own staging company, European Grid Systems, which has provided the stage not only for U2 but also for other major acts including David Bowie and Stevie Wonder.

Under a Bloody Wet Sky.

U2 The Unforgettable Fire

U2 *Unforgettable Eno*

When you're hot you're boiling.
After *WAR* U2 could do no wrong. A
hit album, two hit singles, Band of the
Year in the 1983 *Rolling Stone
Critics' Poll*, and sell-out concerts in
America and Japan. The world was
their oyster.

Yet the band were at a crossroads;
they still hadn't found what they were
looking for. Which is why they sought
the master of ambience (electronic
muzak to the unenlightened), Brian
Eno.

Eno first found fame and fortune with
Brian Ferry and Roxy Music. While
Ferry was the voice and look of the
band, Eno contributed a series of
assorted electronic bleeps and noises.
Some people talk to their plants; Eno
talked to his synthesisers, his custom
built offspring.

After much persuasion he joined U2
at Slane Castle in County Meath to
produce *The Unforgettable Fire* with
his French Canadian collaborator
Daniel Lanois.

In between takes he sipped
peppermint tea. Some people felt he
was very strange but most thought he
was extremely hip.

He was the ideal producer for the new
U2 album.

The Unforgettable Fire was a radical departure for U2. Peter Rowen wasn't on the cover.

Instead there was a snap of Moydrum Castle, County Westmeath. The setting was very ambient. The title came from a grimmer landscape however: a collection of paintings by the survivors of the nuclear nightmare at Hiroshima and Nagasaki.

(When U2 played in Dublin in June '85 they brought over some of the paintings for an exhibition in an arts centre in the city.)

In August '84 the band started a world tour in New Zealand. They headed for Australia the following month playing to more than 30,000 fans in Melbourne. By the time they left Australia to return to Europe they had four albums in the Australian charts.

In September, *Pride (In The Name Of Love)*, the first single to be released from the album, reached number three in the UK charts, the band's highest single chart placing to date.

It also earned the band their first ever silver disc for a single.

The following month *The Unforgettable Fire* hit the racks and soared straight to the top of the UK album charts. Meanwhile *Pride* had gone to number one in Australia, the band's first number one single outside Ireland.

They ended the year playing two shows in the Wembley Arena, London, and then headed back to the east coast of America, finishing with two concerts in Los Angeles and San Francisco.

It was to be three years before U2 released another album. Meanwhile there were things to do, places to see.

U2 *Mum's Not the Word*

Kids. You bear them, you rear them but in the end they're nothing but trouble.

As early as '81 Bono announced that U2 wanted to set up their own record label. In August '84 Mother Records was launched.

It seemed like a good idea at the time. Take some young unrecorded bands under your wing, let them make a single and wait for a big label to snap them up and make megabucks.

Some of the Mother children went on to make their way in the big bad world and stand on their own feet. The Hothouse Flowers were one of the success stories.

But for every Mother success there was a disgruntled band anxious to tell anybody who would listen how rotten U2 were.

One band complained that Mother had promised to put out singles and then changed its mind.

But the most savage attack on the label came from ex-Boomtown Rats and Bananarama manager, Fachtna Ó Ceallaigh, who was hired by U2 as the label's manager in October '85. A year later they fired him after he made this outburst in an uninhibited interview:

" . . . I literally despise the music U2 make. Obviously I was highly attracted by the theory of the label, and very attracted by the fact that they were going to pay me wages because I haven't had any money for

"He takes after his mother."

the previous two years."
He went on:
"There's this kind of 'God Almighty' approach to U2 in Ireland that's really distressing. There's this aura of correctness about everything U2 does and people tend not to question or to argue the point. And I don't think that's right."
After his departure from Mother, Ó Ceallaigh went on to manage bald chanteuse Sinead O'Connor.
She had collaborated with The Edge on a song called *Heroine*, but she wasn't very happy with U2 either.
"They have fingers in every pie — they f***ing rule Dublin," she bleated. "There's not a band in Dublin who could get anywhere if

they weren't in some way associated with U2."
Today Mother is managed by former showband drummer, Dave Pennefather, with Larry supervising its operations for the band. Larry says that Mother is not a charity. They want the label to be self-financing.
"It's not a money making thing . . . it is basically U2 trying to give younger bands a hand. There's not one chance that we've ripped people off or that we've held people to bad deals and anyone who says that is a liar."
The new, re-organised Mother has changed policy. No longer does it concentrate exclusively on unrecorded bands. In fact two of its

latest signings — The Stars of Heaven and The Golden Horde — have spent years playing to well-deserved critical acclaim and tragically unmerited commercial apathy.

U2 *America (or Amerika)*

Like the surfboard, the hamburger, Mickey Mouse, Ronald Reagan, the Harley Davidson motorbike, Bruce Springsteen and the Empire State building, U2 are now an American institution.

As early as 1981 Adam Clayton told an interviewer: "We actually enjoy America. We're not here to slag it off or say America stinks and they don't listen to good music."

By '83, U2 were already playing to audiences of 10,000 people a night as they started playing their first stadium gigs. In April '83 they got a gold record for sales of *WAR*.

In May '87 *Time* called them "Rock's Hottest Ticket".

And sales of concert tickets in the US in '87 revealed that more Americans had flocked to see U2 than any other band. They grossed a staggering £18 million in ticket sales, more than Bon Jovi, Pink Floyd, The Grateful Dead, David Bowie, Motley Crue and Whitney Houston among others.

It was at this time that Bono was developing his thesis of the two Americas.

"America both fascinates me and frightens me," he mused. "I can't get it out of my system. The German film maker Wim Wenders, who directed *Paris Texas*, has said that America

has colonised our unconscious. He's right. America is everywhere. You don't even have to go there — it comes to you. No matter where we live it's pumped into our homes in Dallas, Dynasty and Hill Street Blues. It's Hollywood, it's Coca-Cola, it's Levis, it's Harley Davidsons."

Bono visited Nicaragua and El Salvador in '87 and was appalled by the effect of American foreign policy on the people living in Central America. "I have two conflicting visions of America. One it's a kind of dream landscape and the other it's a kind of black comedy."

U2 discover the Joshua Tree

U2 rustle up some sales

U2 *Huge*

"The thought of the world waiting for an LP called *The Joshua Tree* is a bit ridiculous," mused a philosophical Bono after they had recorded their fifth studio album.

By December '87 the album had sold 12 million copies.

The Joshua Tree tour started in Tempe, Arizona, and ran for 264 days.

They played 110 shows in 72 venues in 15 countries selling 3,160,918 tickets.

With Or Without You gave the band their first number 1 single in the States. *I Still Haven't Found What I'm Looking For* repeated its success. And in April '87 U2 were on the cover of *Time* . . . an honour conferred on only two Irishmen previously — Bob Geldof and Dr Garret FitzGerald. Then it was back to Dublin to play their first Irish concert in two years. In August Bono was voted one of the ten sexiest men in the world by *Playgirl* magazine; he ranked with other macho megahunks like Tom Cruise and Rupert Murdoch.

"At the end of '87," opined one English rock critic, "U2 might just be the biggest rock'n'roll band on the planet."

63

"Bono will call you back. He's busy rehearsing right now."

U2 *Writing on the Wall*

When Bono launched an impromptu "Save The Yuppie" public concert in the heart of San Francisco during the *Joshua Tree* tour, he was surprised that many people did not get the joke. The city's mayor was surprised, too, when the muse descended on Bono, moving him to spray "Stop The Traffic, Rock and Roll" on a huge concrete fountain.

"They don't like graffiti in San Francisco — they have a 600 dollar reward for anyone who hands in a graffiti artist," Bono reflected after he was charged with malicious mischief.

The charge was later dropped and the sculptor who created the fountain joined U2 on stage at a subsequent gig saying it was okay by him if Bono wanted to spray his statue.

And to show that there were no hard feelings he sprayed "Rock'n'Roll stops the madness" onstage.

"He was a right headbanger actually," The Edge recalled later.

But thousands of miles away the Lord Mayor of Dublin, Carmencita Hederman, was not amused. "It is a terribly bad example for his fans and I would urge all followers of U2 not to copy what he may have done in a moment of spontaneous enthusiasm," she told a reporter.

That didn't stop U2 devotees heading to Windmill Lane to spray endearments such as "Italy Loves U2" and "Edge I think you're Brill" on the studio walls.

U2 *The Lost Generation*

At the age of 25 Bono heard his first John Lee Hooker record. "We were part of the lost generation after punk," he lamented. "Our musical life began with *Marquee Moon* (Television) and *Horses* (Patti Smith)."

More revelations followed: Willie Nelson, Scott Walker, Elvis Presley, Buddy Holly, Johnny Cash, Bob Dylan, Van Morrison. Soon Bono & Co. were swopping licks and ideas with the likes of Bob Dylan, BB King, Roy Orbison, Van the Man and even Keith Richards.

How could Bono reconcile Richards's tempestuous rock'n'roll lifestyle with his own?

"Admit it — you've been jamming with that Keith Richards again."

Bono discovers the Blues.

"If Keith was 20 years old in the Eighties I don't think he would have got into junk, he wouldn't have been into heroin as rebellion. The Sixties were a different time and in terms of rock'n'roll it was the first time."

"People were dizzy with it and maybe it seemed the right thing to do at the time or whatever. But it is obvious it was the wrong thing to do because a lot of people died. Now we know that but then they didn't."

In the Sixties and Seventies, the Stones paid their dues to the great rhythm and blues legends. U2 made a similar act of homage with *Rattle and Hum* at the end of the Eighties.

Bono explained, "As an Irishman, I feel a real closeness to the black man

U2 discover traditional Irish music.

because we were both the underdog, because we both have soul and the spirit to spit it out, because we both are too raw to sit nicely on the stiff upper lip of the intelligentsia wherever they may be found in art circles. The Irish have been described as white niggers and I take that as a compliment."

Bono recalled that he had grown up on the The Dubliners — arguably Ireland's most popular traditional group — but had forsaken them to groove with David Bowie and Patti Smith instead.

Yet when The Dubliners celebrated their 25th anniversary on television in March '87, U2 were among those who paid their respects.

"Your dentures, Mr. MacGowan."

Dunphy at Milwall.

The Unforgettable Ire

"Bono laughed and said, 'You're f***ing rat poison, aren't you.'" The subject of this endearment was Eamon Dunphy, author of the official U2 biography, *Unforgettable Fire*. Dunphy had played professional soccer for 17 years with Milwall, Manchester United, York, Charlton and Reading. When he returned to Ireland in '77 he spent a few years with Shamrock Rovers before turning his hand to sports writing.

He quickly became one of the highest paid journalists around, revered and loathed for his no-holds-barred attacks on everything and everyone that affronted him. His muse ranged from sports to politics, media, history and sociology.

"They're portraits of Eamon Dunphy."

In '85 he met Paul McGuinness in a Dublin night club. McGuinness asked him to write something about U2. Dunphy had never heard of the band — he thought McGuinness was referring to UB 40! McGuinness later asked him to write the official U2 biography. He agreed to do it provided he was given complete access to the band and they would have no veto on the finished product.

Dunphy wanted to call the book *Suburban Heroes* but wiser council prevailed.

At first he found it hard to find a publisher. But the book went on to become a bestseller and probably made Dunphy more money than he had earned in his entire soccer career.

However it got mixed reviews from the critics and even a discreet thumbs down from U2.

After the band publicly criticised the work he retorted, "They wanted my book to be a kind of picture book but with all the hassle since it was published I could write another bestseller about the whole affair."

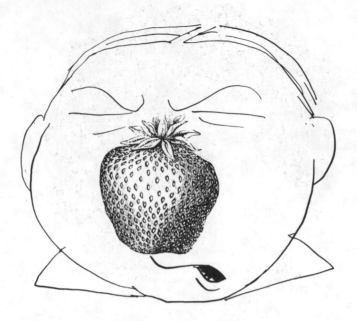

Strawberry Fields Forever!

Bob Dylan, a protégé of U2.

"Sorry. There ain't no cure for the
summertime blues."

"Yep. Them's the original blue suede shoes the King himself wore."

U2 *Rattle & Humdinger*

It started with Philip Joanou, a protegé of Stephen Spielberg. In '87 he was asked to make a U2 film which could be screened worldwide to give fans who hadn't seen them play live a glimpse of life on the road with the hottest band on the planet.

Rattle And Hum was filmed between September '87 and July '88 in Dublin and America.

"Bono was fabulous," recalled Joanou. "Know what he wanted me to do? He wanted to pull the limo over to the curbside, find some U2 punter, haul him inside and take him to the show. Can you imagine that?

Unfortunately we were on Park Avenue at the time."

The film had its world première in October '88 at Dublin's Savoy Cinema. This was attended by anybody who was anybody in Irish society.

Before the première the band played an impromptu 20 minute concert outside the cinema.

Afterwards Irish President, Patrick Hillery, confided to a gossip columnist, "I play them at full blast in Áras an Uachtaráin (the presidential headquarters) bopping around all the time. In fact I often wonder whether

people strolling outside appreciate what they're hearing. Should I have my system amplified through the whole Park do you think?"

The film got mixed reviews. *The Sunday Times* film critic described it as "possibly the worst rock documentary ever made". *Melody Maker* said it was "the outstanding rock film of our time".

The album was a major hit, selling over five million copies worldwide. U2 released *Desire* as a single and got their first British No 1 after eight years of near misses.

U2 *Keats and Bono*

As a teenager, Bono had a lot of time for John Keats. English classes were interesting. "Keats was a drug, his excess was success at 16 in my efforts to sit closer to Maeve O'Regan . . . he sort of stuck us together."

So Bono told the literary magazine, Poetry Ireland. The journal asked various celebs who their favourite poets were. Topping Bono's list were Donne, Shelley, Byron, Clarke and Kinsella.

He had great respect for Yeats, too. He feared him like God "because they dressed the same." However the most influential bard was the American Emily Dickinson.

Nowadays one of Bono's favourite rhymesters is Charles Bukowski. He also likes the short stories of Raymond Carver and the plays of Tenessee Williams.

Great Rock comebacks # 1: The Who

U2 *Rock of ages*

"Hope I die before I get old," bellowed a defiant Roger Daltrey on The Who's megahit, *My Generation*. Perhaps fortunately, that death wish has not been granted.

Twenty four years later The Who were back on the road with a 'reunion' tour, a little older, a little wiser and a little richer.

The Eighties ended with the revenge of the wrinklies. Paul McCartney, Crosby, Stills etc, etc, Pink Floyd, Yes and The Rolling Stones all came back and wallowed in pots of money. The touts had a field day with front row seats for the Stones' US shows fetching $200, Who tickets going for $275 and McCartney tickets raising a stupendous $500 to $600.

The spectacle of all these fortysomethings prancing about on stage gave pause for thought. It raised a very large question. And Mick Jagger answered that question. Why were they doing it?

"Money. That's the simplistic answer. Why are they getting money? Because people are willing to come and see them."

Great Rock comebacks # 2: Crosby, Stills, Nash & Young

81

"Just the sticks, you moron!"

U2 *Metal Gurus*

They are the prehistoric monsters of rock, purveyors of long and greasy hair, tight leather trousers and 15 minute drum solos.

Bands like Cinderella, Vixen, Megadeth, Motley Crue, Anthrax and Dogs D'Amour laugh at Satan and spit in his face. And they laugh even louder and longer at the critics and "real" rock music fans who detest and abhor everything they stand for. Because Heavy Metal will never die. Musical juggernauts, mowing down anyone who dares stand in their path, they have declared a war of attrition on the wimps and pretty boys who call themselves pop stars. On stage they strut their stuff and drink the blood of headless chickens.

On the other hand, you also have Bon Jovi whose *Slippery and Wet* album has already sold 14 million copies, the acceptable face of Heavy Metal, perhaps even bigger than U2.

"I said, 20 years of playing heavy metal music has impaired your hearing."

"There's a glitch in the laser system."

**FREE !!! NAME YOUR OWN
METAL BAND!**
**Instructions: Take one word from
Column A and combine with a
suitable word from Column B.**

Column A	Column B
Scorched	Dogs
Black	Rats
Mega	Snake
Foul	Doom
Vile	Warriors
Wasted	Reaper
Bad	Sage
Raging	Wizard
Savage	Experience
Crippled	Torment
Grym	Mission
Silver	Quest
Iron	Dragon
Pink	Hounds
Purple	Angels
Screaming	Massacre
Pussy	Revenge
Sleazy	Boys
Sweet	Kiss
Rich	Shamen
Knight	Fist
Deviant	Rose
Toy	Taboo
Brutal	Squad
Free	Doll
Young	Love Machine
Demented	Cats
Shock	Steel
Thunder	Metal
Psycho	Youth
Baneful	Obscenity
Brass	Blood
Sex	Horse
Dedd	Factory
Excresence	Destroyer

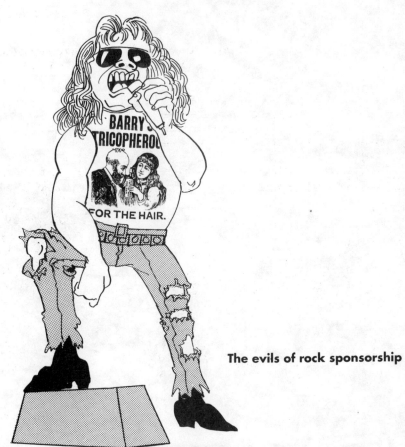

The evils of rock sponsorship

85

 Mother Earth

Greenpeace is a recent signing to the Mother label. In June, the double album, *Rainbow Warriors*, which features 31 tracks from ecologically sound rockers got its Irish release courtesy of Mum.

The non-profit compilation had already sold over 1 million copies in the USSR. The Edge and Adam Clayton showed up at a launch to boost Hibernian sales.

"We have always been supporters of Greenpeace because they are the only people sticking their necks out and taking the initiative on Sellafield and not the Irish Government," the Edge revealed.

The least successful
rapper in the world

U2 *Epilogue . . .*

Ali had a baby called Jordan in May
'89. Two months later she got a degree
in Social Science from University
College Dublin. Bono told reporters
his daughter would probably be
something like a rocket scientist, a
politician or a removal truck driver.
Meanwhile Dave and Aisling had their
third child, a baby girl called Blue.
Paul McGuinness was drawing up
plans for Ireland's first independent
television company while Larry was
keeping an eye on some of the new
additions to the Mother family.
In August Chris Blackwell sold Island
Records to Polygram for an estimated
£300 million. There were some
rumours that U2 had made around
£30 million from the deal as a result
of an 11 per cent share they had
taken out in the company in lieu of
royalties.
Adam became an Irish citizen making
a Declaration of Fidelity at
Rathfarnham District Court in
County Dublin in February. In
September he made another court
appearance — this time at Dundrum
District Court where he pleaded
guilty to possessing cannabis resin at
the Blue Light pub, Glencullen,
County Dublin on 6 August '89.
He was ordered to pay £25,000 to the
Dublin Women's Aid refuge for
battered wives and given the
Probation Act after his solicitor
pointed out that a conviction could
detrimentally affect his chances of
getting visas for future U2 tours.

**"For the next eight hours I'll be bringing
you an in-depth analysis of world politics . . . "**

Two weeks later Adam set off with the
rest of the band on a tour of
Australia, Japan and New Zealand.
As 1989 drew to a close U2 were still
the biggest band in the world. Only
Stock, Aitken and Waterman and
their Larry Mullen lookalikes Bros
stood in their way commercially.
Artistically, Prince was still the Joker
in the pack.
The depressingly ubiquitous SAW had
no time for U2.
"The three minute pop song is not a
place for politics," said Mike Stock.
"It's disrespectful, facile. Take U2. *I
Still Haven't Found What I'm
Looking For* is a song about him

finding his God but the kids out there
buy it under the impression it's a love
song. The problem is that kids are
terribly influenced by pop and U2
manipulate that."
Which probably means that Bono and
Kylie Minogue won't be doing any
duets in the future.
Meanwhile, at this very moment, in a
dingy little basement somewhere in
the Western Hemisphere, an
undiscovered four piece is hatching
its masterplan, dreaming of becoming
the next U2 . . .

"Oh no! Some @*!!* has sampled my stereo!"

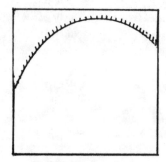

Phil Collins's scalp

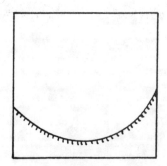

George Michael's chin.

"It's okay — I'm a rock promoter."

"You're suffering from heavy metal fatigue."

Bono's third farewell solo tour, 2010 A.D.

U2 — a new release in 2040 A.D.